GOD'S WAR CHEST

Destined To Become The Lord's Secret Weapon

Paula Vignali

West Orange, New Jersey

No part of this publication may be reproduced, stored in a retrieval system, or transmitted in any form or by any means, electronic, mechanical, photocopying, recording, scanning, or otherwise, except as permitted under Section 107 or 108 of the 1976 United States Copyright Act, without either the prior written permission of the Publisher, or authorization through payment of the appropriate per-copy fee to the Copyright Clearance Center, Inc., 222 Rosewood Drive, Danvers, MA 01923, (978) 750-8400, fax (978) 646-8600, or on the web at www.copyright.com.
Requests to the Publisher for permission should be addressed to the Permission Department, Blue Magic Publishing, Inc.; PO Box 24, Williamstown, NJ 08094, 888-237-6101 (toll free/fax), or online at http://www.bluemagicpublishing.com

Copyright 2011 © by Paula Vignali
All rights reserved.
Published by Blue Magic Publishing, Inc. Williamstown, New Jersey.
Booked edited by : Sological Underpennings
For general information on our other products and services or for technical support, please contact our Customer Care Department at 888-237-6101 (toll-free/fax).
Vignali, Paula.
God's War Chest / Paula Vignali.
ISBN 978-0-9707915-9-7
Library of Congress Control Number: 2011908850

Dedication

With Love from the Father.

Dedicated to my seed and seeds seed henceforth and forever. Dominic, Alexandria, Marisa, Nicholas, Vincent, Isabella, Stephanie and Michael.

About The Author

Biography

As a seasoned minster of the Gospel, Paula Vignali has an appeal that transcends barriers of age, culture and denomination. For more than 33 years Paula has served in the ministry as an elder and teacher replete with a prophetic anointing. Paula has directly impacted the lives of many with her God-inspired message of hope and healing.

Paula Vignali's ministry is headquartered in Bedminster, New Jersey. Her services include ministry training, workshops, seminars, keynotes and the creation and distribution of ministry-based information products.

Paula is a proud wife of 47 years of marriage with 3 children and 8 grandchildren.

Preface

In 1987, the Lord told me that He wanted me to train His people for war. He said, "We are no longer sending the fearful home, but as with Gideon, we are at the waters of decision to determine who is skilled for war. He continued, "They cannot war if they do not understand righteousness. Teach their hands to war." God taught me it is imperative that we understand our righteousness, our identity in Christ and the awesomeness of our all-sufficient, ever-present God! He has been and always will be enough to overcome evil. It is now twenty-five years later and we are still in the same place we were in 1987. God is speaking the same command to a new generation. What happened to the church that stifled their entrance into the plan of God? The church must walk circumspect and understand why God sees fit to rehearse in our ears the areas of failure that plagued so many before us. We seem to lose sight of the goal. The church, like Eve, is easily distracted from her purpose. My goal is to build soldiers for this army who will not be consumed with the affairs of this life. God took the land with three-hundred of Gideon's MEN OF WAR. These were men of humility, obedience, spiritual focus and loyalty to God. We must not allow this move of God to pass us by again. I believe the Word holds the answer.

Even as a child the desire to write and proclaim God's goodness was ever present. Going through the many stages of life and experiencing His wonderful mercies through times of tribulations, has caused me to know His voice better and better. The still small voice of my Savior gnawed away at me to put on paper for all to see His marvelous promise fulfilled in my life. As a student of the Holy Ghost, I was hidden away with Him for many years as He brought me off a death bed.

At the age of 29, the doctors gave me a glim prospect for a long life. The circumstances drove me to seek the giver of life to find the answer of the ages in His Word. WHY WAS I HERE? In that I found a beautiful relationship with an ever present, loving Faithful God. One who not only told me why I was here, but how to live life abundantly. My desire is that you come away with fresh revelation, understanding who you are, who God is and who we war against.

This book is for all who seek a city whose builder and maker is God and desire to walk out their destiny in victory. I appreciate the fact that the Word of God has given me the privilege to live my life to the fullest with my husband of almost 50 years. To raise three wonderful faith-filled children and experience the joy of eight grandchildren, all of whom I adore.

INTRODUCTION

Over twenty years after the initial revelation, God's plan began to manifest. One day, my Pastor called and asked if he could see me. When he arrived, he talked about the church's new building project. He wanted to know if I would participate in the capital campaign and be responsible for raising the finances for the building. While I had participated in building projects in the past, I had never been responsible for collections. This was a new challenge.

I agreed to pray and do whatever he needed to be done. As we gathered during our preparation time, I asked the Lord for guidance. One Sunday it was my turn to address the congregation regarding their giving. The Lord instructed me to bring in a chest as a symbol which He called a WAR CHEST. While I prayed about this, the Lord told me to get an army camouflage trunk and dress in khakis. The speech I prepared became a military charge for His people to recognize the seriousness of this project. It wasn't just another building, because "we" are His building. Our new church would be a place of transition for the next move of God.

Pursuant to the charge I presented to the congregation that day, my Pastors asked me to teach a class on the concept of the war chest. I prepared the material given to me by the Holy Spirit for that class, much of which is shared within the pages of this book.

We must now prepare for war, not only for the battles, but for the victory.

Contents

Dedication

About The Author

Preface

Introduction

Obedience, The Fruit Of Faith...11

In His Presence...23

God's Secret Weapons..37

Identity Theft..43

Who Are We?...55

You Can't Kill A Dead Man...63

The Storehouse Of Special Wealth...73

Notes...83

Quick Order Forms...88

Chapters

Obedience, the Fruit of Faith

In His Presence

God's Secret Weapons

Identity Theft

Who Are We?

You Can't Kill a Dead Man

The Storehouse of Special Wealth

Chapter 1
Obedience, the Fruit of Faith

I will prepare Him a habitation: My father's God and I will exalt Him. The Lord is a man of war; the Lord of Hosts is His name."

Exodus 15:3

When God first gave me the concept of the war chest, I thought, "Lord, war chest?" As I searched for meaning, Webster's dictionary revealed that a war chest is "a fund to finance a war." The Lord deepened the revelation for me with this:

A calculating of the necessities for the venture, in a time of preparation.

He directed me to Luke 14:28-31.

"For which of you, intending to build a tower, does not sit down first and count the cost, whether he has enough to finish it lest, after he has laid the foundation, and is not able to finish, all who see it begin to mock him, saying, 'This man began to build and was not able to finish'? Or what king, going to make war against another king, does not sit down first and consider whether he is able with ten thousand to meet him who comes against him with twenty thousand?"

In these verses, Jesus was talking about the cost, or assessment of what it takes to complete a project. Whether it is your commitment to God, building a house, or going to war, we need to assess if we have what it takes to finish. Like Paul, we should be able to say, "I ran the race, I finished the course" (2 Timothy 4:7). We all want to hear the Lord say, "Well done thy good and faithful servant" (Matthew 25:23).

This means that when you have a God-given task to complete, you, much like Gideon and his men, must take stock of your heart. The Lord told Gideon to lead his people to war even though their enemy was great in number. Then the Lord cut the number of Gideon's troops to three-hundred men who met God's qualifications as true warriors. Do you have what it takes to move forward in battle? Are your eyes open and focused on the Lord or are you focused only on what you think you need? We can't be like Israel, who wanted to be like the world, and cried "give us a king," because they desired to have what they wanted. We must seek God on our faces in order to discover the pitfalls of previous generations and align ourselves with God and His Word. God has already anticipated all the necessities for your victory, prior to your creation. There is no need to be anxious over how it will be accomplished because the Lord will supply.

Chapter 1 : Obedience, the Fruit of Faith

The great revivals of the 19th and 20th centuries manifested a fresh move of God's power in men and woman who took the time to know God and hear His voice. But, as with every great move of God, something infiltrated the church to derail her. The church succumbed to temptation and relegated herself to the commonality of the world. She was seduced by doctrines of devils and let the Word of Righteousness slip from her consciousness. Holy understanding was clouded by sin. They were like the man who looks in a mirror and recognizes himself, but forgets what he looks like after he turns away from it. As the healing revivals of the 1940s and 50s came to a close, a movement of faith emerged on the scene. This move of God brought life back to the Church through the Word of God and unveiled the WILL of God's love for them. It unveiled His will to have them take dominion and rule in this life. It didn't take long for the enemy to pervert the move of the Spirit. Before long the body was no different than the church at Corinth. Sexual sin, competition, envy, strife and an overzealous sense of pride (Phariseeism) grieved the Holy Spirit and hindered the move. This generation looked at the world with natural eyes, and ignorant of Satan's devices, they fashioned themselves after the world. Our kingdom is in the spirit and **our economic system** consists of the faith-filled Words of God.

The Bible says that without faith it is impossible to please God (Hebrews 11:6). It requires faith and a steadfast belief in God to go forth in battle when you do not know the details, the expected outcome or even the full strategy. As demonstrated many times in His Word, God does not always reveal the full

God's War Chest

plan from the start; His desire is that we obey His instructions and trust Him to handle the rest.

Obedience is the fruit of faith. For when you plant God's word in your heart, and water it with your words, that faith act is a manifestation of your obedience. Faith allows you to rest on the Word of the Lord, trusting that if He said it, He will bring it to pass.

"And now, Israel, what does the LORD your God require of you, but to fear the LORD your God, to walk in all His ways and to love Him, to serve the LORD your God with all your heart and with all your soul, and to keep the commandments of the LORD and His statutes which I command you today for your good? Indeed heaven and the highest heavens belong to the LORD your God, also the earth with all that is in it." (Deuteronomy 10:12-14)

By His Word the stars are held in place, and to His Word the wind and sea submit; even the unclean spirits obey His Word. The only part of creation that doesn't obey God is man. Because God created us in His image and likeness, man alone has free will.

Choice

"Choose for yourselves this day who you will serve…but for me and my house we will serve the Lord" (Joshua 24:15).

I don't think Christians realize the importance of choice. We have been seduced by religion into thinking our decision for Christ was the end of the story, when it is the powerful beginning. Through the decisions we make EVERYDAY, we

Chapter 1 : Obedience, the Fruit of Faith

choose whether we will agree with the Word or not. It says in the book of Romans:

"Neither yield ye your members as instruments of unrighteousness unto sin: but yield yourselves unto God, as those that are alive from the dead, and your members as instruments of righteousness unto God. **For sin shall not have dominion over you: for ye are not under the law, but under grace.** What then? Shall we sin, because we are not under the law, but under grace? God forbid. **Know ye not, that to whom ye yield yourselves servants to obey, his servants ye are to whom ye obey; whether of sin unto death, or of obedience unto righteousness?** To whom you yield your members to obey that's whose servant you become. (Romans 6:13-16)"

In Genesis, Adam and Eve made a CHOICE to disobey God. The Word says afterwards they hid themselves because they were naked and made themselves aprons of fig leaves. They attempted to cover their shame. Sin will always cause you to hide from God.

Fig leaves represent anything we do to cover our nakedness and shame. We all have fig leaves, for example: status, degrees, intellectualism, style, morality or anything we hide behind to prove we're not defective, broken, or sinful. They come in many different forms, but they have two things in common: THEY ARE SELF-MADE and THEY ARE SELF-COVERING. Our right standing with God has nothing to do with our works and everything to do with the BLOOD OF JESUS.

Adam and Eve must have felt the fig leaves were inadequate to cover their sin because they ran and hid when they heard God in the garden. Eden was a garden of delight with protection and provision. However, Adam and Eve allowed the enemy to plant seeds of fear that something was missing in their lives because they were not eating the fruit of one particular tree. Although God told them not to eat the fruit of that tree, they were deceived and were enticed to disobey God.

Fear results in choosing what the enemy says over what God says! Fear is reacting to the situations of life outside of the Word. Fear is the antithesis of FAITH. If obedience is the fruit of faith, the fruit of fear is disobedience. Fear is in direct opposition to God and the root of our failing to receive what God has for us. Fear is the result of sin consciousness, for example: I didn't pray enough, I didn't give enough, I'm not good enough. Fear is an awareness of OUR shortcomings.

Adam and Eve's disobedience brought separation in the spirit, soul and body. Spiritually, their intimate relationship with God was severed; they were no longer in His Presence, face to face. Sin and death were introduced to their souls and replaced God's life within them. Their bodies would eventually return to dust. Adam and Eve's disobedience brought death in every aspect of their existence.

However, God did not leave Adam and Eve to die in their sin. He made them a covering using animal's skin (Genesis 3:21). "Wesley's commentary says these coats of skin had significance. Up to that point, there had been no death. The beasts whose skins they used had to be slain before their eyes so that they would see death. Thus, the first creature to die was a sacrifice for their sins, a figure of Christ, representing our need for a deliverer.

Chapter 1 : Obedience, the Fruit of Faith

Trusting God

In Judges 1 we read how the people of Israel did not drive out the enemies who lived in the land God had given them. Instead of driving out the enemies, they made a deal with them. The Word says God has given us the authority and given us dominion over the land of our souls. The enemies we fight are in our emotions. These enemies are complacency, dullness of hearing, fear and doubt. We see how the disobedience of God's people caused their enemies to prevail over them and drove them into hiding in dens and caves. As seen with Adam and Eve, disobedience drives the people of God into hiding.

But once again, God did not simply leave the people to die. For example, in Judges 6:11, the Angel of the Lord appeared to Gideon as he was in the winepress threshing wheat, to hide the crop from the enemy. I heard it said that Gideon was afraid so that's why he was hiding. On the contrary, I believe Gideon had courage to gather the wheat and cunningly threshed it where the enemy wouldn't look.

The Angel of the Lord said, "The Lord is with thee, oh mighty man of valor." Gideon said, "Oh my Lord, if the Lord be with us then why is all this befallen us? And where art all the miracles our fathers told us about?" This sounds like those of us who live with unfavorable circumstances and wonder when God will show up.

The Lord looked upon him and said, "Go in this thy might and thou shall save Israel from the Midianites. Have not I sent thee?" Then, doubting what the Lord had spoken, Gideon told him that his family was poor and he was the least in his father's house.

Gideon's reaction was similar to how many of us would have responded. The Lord tells us to do something and we automatically think of our inability.

This reminds me of a time when I was in a grocery store shopping. As I walked down the aisle, I saw a man with an amputated leg. The Lord spoke to me and said "Go over to him and command his leg to grow." My first thought was, I can't do this! Automatically, one million thoughts flooded my mind. **FEAR gripped me!** I thought, "How can I do this?" I went over to him and started to talk to him and his wife about the Lord. I told him about Jesus and how He heals, about salvation and what a great church I had, and asked if I could pray for him. He agreed. BUT I NEVER COMMANDED THE LEG TO GROW. As soon as I walked out of the store the Lord said to me, "Did I ask you to make it grow? NO! I told you to command it to grow and I WOULD DO THE REST."

We forget that it's not up to us to make it happen. We just need to be full of courage and obedient to what He says. When our knowledge of God increases, we understand that He has it under control; all we have to do is trust Him and obey His word. Centuries have come and gone, but doctrines and denominations have done nothing but cloud the real issue which is KNOWING GOD. For when you know God, you can trust Him, and when you trust Him you can REST!

Gideon did not understand that his "might" or ability was that the Lord was **with him.** He said to the Lord, "If I've found grace in your sight show me a sign and don't leave until I can

Chapter 1 : Obedience, the Fruit of Faith

present thee with a gift." He prepared the flesh of a young goat and unleavened cakes. He placed the meat in a basket and the broth in a pot and presented it to the Angel of the Lord.

The Angel said, "Take the flesh and the bread and lay it on the ROCK and pour out the broth." Then the Angel of the Lord put forth the staff in his hand touched the flesh and the cakes and a fire rose up out of the rock and consumed the sacrifice. When we present ourselves as a living sacrifice, He touches us with His scepter of righteousness, and the Holy Ghost Fire consumes us. I see that as a foreshadowing of our lives as saints in total surrender to Christ; the fire of the Holy Ghost consumes us, the offering, so that there is nothing left of us, but our ability in Him. I said all that to say;

When He prepared the sacrifice, the fire fell.

Are you a prepared sacrifice?

Holy fire only comes with our commitment and passion for the things of God. When Gideon prepared the sacrifice, indicating his desire to please God, the fire fell. Gideon went on to lead God's people to victory because of his obedience. We have to stop looking for outward manifestations and let the Zeal of God consume us.

The Word says we are to present our bodies as living sacrifices, holy, acceptable unto God, which is our reasonable service. (Romans 12:1)

Chapters

Obedience, the Fruit of Faith

In His Presence

God's Secret Weapons

Identity Theft

Who Are We?

You Can't Kill a Dead Man

The Storehouse of Special Wealth

Chapter 2

In His Presence

It is time to **prepare our hearts** for the habitation of the LORD. The Word says, "They that know their God will be strong and do great exploits." This Scripture is talking about an end time army: men and women covenanted with the Lord Jesus Christ and the Father God, who allow the <u>Holy Spirit His true place of leadership in their lives and through His Word have come to KNOW and Trust Him.</u>

One morning when I awoke, I mused over things the Lord had spoken to me in a dream. In this dream, I had a conversation with the Lord during which He told me we obtain victory over the enemy when we perceive situations the way God sees them.

We need to go to Him and SEEK HIS FACE until we get the answer. That's the example we see in the Word. The trouble is in trying to assimilate the spiritual by using our natural senses and emotions. God is saying "Look at it from my point of view, from the spirit, from the eternal."

When Adam and Eve sinned, they were ashamed and hid themselves from the presence of God when they heard the voice of the Lord in the garden (Genesis 3:8-9).

This word presence in verse 8 is the first occurrence of the Hebrew word 'PANIYM' and means a face to face relationship; it's that intimate place that endues you with the power and authority that comes only from HIS PRESENCE. That is exactly what Lucifer LOST in his rebellion to God.

"And they heard the voice of the Lord walking in the garden in the cool of the day and Adam and his wife hid themselves from the PRESENCE (paniym) of the Lord amongst the trees in the garden." (Genesis 3:8)

The Lord called to Adam and said "Where are you?" This is a rhetorical question, similar to when He asked Elijah in I Kings 19:9, "What are you doing here?" If the Tree of Life in the Garden of Eden was **God's presence**, we are looking at this all wrong. His voice or presence is always speaking. **God wasn't just stopping by.** They were partaking of God's presence and Words on a daily basis. God's desire has always been that we KNOW HIM and partake of His presence.

Why was Eve distracted from the presence of God and The Tree of Life? Was it because her face was toward the other tree? Adam and Eve tried to hide themselves from the presence of the Lord when they disobeyed Him. Their relationship with God had changed. No longer were they the guards of the garden. They were removed from His Presence the same way Lucifer was kicked out of Heaven and the Lord's covering was no longer their garments.

In Genesis 4 we see the same word again, but translated differently. In the story of Cain and Abel, Cain was a farmer and

Abel a shepherd. Both brought an offering but Abel's was accepted and Cain's wasn't. We all have heard teaching on why Cain's offering was not accepted.

I am not interested in why it wasn't accepted, but I am interested in what happened when it wasn't! Genesis 4:5 says, "but unto Cain and his offering He had not respect, and Cain was very angry and his **countenance** fell." That word **countenance** is another occurrence of the word that is translated in Hebrew as "Paniym" meaning "face to face relationship." Cain's face to face relationship with God was severed.

In verse 13 Cain said to the Lord, "my punishment is greater than I can bear, thou hast driven me out this day from the face of the earth and from **Thy face (Paniym)** shall I be hid." His intimate relationship with the Lord was severed.

From the Word of God, we learn that it is necessary to have a face-to-face relationship with the Lord. What you behold is what you become. Moses saw God when **he switched his focus and turned aside to see the bush that burned but was not consumed.** When King Hezekiah was sick, Isaiah told him to get his house in order for he would die. The Word says Hezekiah **turned his face to the wall and prayed to the Lord.** We have to do the same. We must turn our faces toward the Lord and rend our hearts, not our garments.

God's desire has always been that men <u>know</u> Him intimately. Hosea 4:1 says, "Hear the word of the Lord ye children of Israel, for the Lord has a controversy with the inhabitants of the land, because there is no truth, nor mercy, nor <u>knowledge of God in the land</u>."

The word "know" is intimate, as when a man and a woman "know" each other. Psalm 34:8 says, "Taste and see that the Lord is good." The word taste translates in Hebrew to perceive and the word see is to know. God's desire has always been that we know Him and have fellowship with Him:

"The Father sent Jesus, "so we might see Him." He gave us His inspired Word that we might hear Him. He sent His Holy Spirit that we might know Him. The church lacks confidence in the reality that we can look in the face of our Savior, take on His Spirit, and have Him furnish us with His presence and anointing to do the job He's called us to do. The world has assimilated the process. As they focus on whatever they worship such as money, power and success, they become what they behold.

We saw this occur in Malachi as the Lord discusses with the priests His displeasure with Israel for their lack of intimacy with Him which caused them to lapse into sin. The priests gave up following the dictates of God and caused many to stumble at the law. God addressed the priests and said, "Where is my honor you that despise my name?" Israel did not show reverence for God or His commands. They became an empty tomb, clanging cymbals, and clouds without water. They were like the church today that takes the world as its model. This is in direct opposition to the warning God gave Israel in Deuteronomy to not look at the people who surrounded them, but to keep their focus on the things of God. God accused the priests of despising His name and robbing Him. The priests asked how they had despised and robbed God. God's response was to tell the priests

Chapter 2: In His Presence

they had robbed Him of their presence and obedience to supply for my people.

"Bring all the tithes into the storehouse that there may be meat in my house."

God's emphasis was on their act of disobedience and their lack of provision in His house.

The prophecy of Malachi was clearly after Haggai and Zechariah. The reconstruction of the temple had been completed long enough for abuses to creep into the sacrificial system. Moreover the spiritual state of the people seems to have been in decline. Divorce was widespread, mixed marriages were contracted for power's sake, and tithes neglected. They had missed the whole point. Their focus had become ritualistic service and they had forsaken their FACE TO FACE relationship with God. A disintegration of their relationship had occurred. Their slothful attitude caused the lack, but God said,

"'Prove me now,' says the Lord of hosts, if I will not open the windows of heaven and pour you out a blessing that there will not be room enough to receive it." (Malachi 3:10)

Prove Him! We prove God's Word by our obedience. His Word says that if we seek first His kingdom and His righteousness, then all these things would be added unto us (Matthew 6:33). The Lord is faithful to perform His Word; all He asks is that we seek Him and **know** Him. His Word speaks to us to reveal His character. It tells us that He watches over His Word to perform it, and that His angels hearken to the Word. It's up to us to bring our thoughts in alignment with His.

God's War Chest

Does your life reflect God's Word, His Covenant at work in you? Deuteronomy 6 explains what the Lord requires of us.

1. "Now these are the commandments, the statutes, and the judgments, which the LORD your God commanded to teach you, that ye might do them in the land whither ye go to possess it:
2. That thou mightest fear the LORD thy God, to keep all his statutes and his commandments, which I command thee, thou, and thy son, and thy son's son, all the days of thy life; and that thy days may be prolonged.
3. Hear therefore, O Israel, and observe to do it; that it may be well with thee, and that ye may increase mightily, as the LORD God of thy fathers hath promised thee, in the land that floweth with milk and honey.
4. Hear, O Israel: The LORD our God is one LORD:
5. And thou shalt love the LORD thy God with all thine heart, and with all thy soul, and with all thy might.
6. And these words, which I command thee this day, shall be in thine heart:
7. And thou shalt teach them diligently unto thy children, and shalt talk of them when thou sittest in thine house, and when thou walkest by the way, and when thou liest down, and when thou risest up.
8. And thou shalt bind them for a sign upon thine hand, and they shall be as frontlets between thine eyes."

In verse 8 the commandment was: "and they (THE WORDS OF GOD) shall be as frontlets between thy eyes." Some Jewish people tie phylacteries (small leather boxes which contain scriptures) to their foreheads. I do not believe God intends for us

Chapter 2: In His Presence

to literally hang His words on our heads. I believe He wants us to allow His instructions to remain in the forefront of our vision like tendrils of hair, so that we view our situations through the Word of God.

The life of Moses exemplifies what it is to live by faith. The sons of Jacob that came to Egypt including Joseph had all died, but their families had increased greatly causing the Egyptians to fear them. In an effort to stop their growth, Pharaoh commanded all midwives to cast the boy babies of the Israelites into the Nile and drown them. The Levites were a tribe of priests whose job it was to minister to the Lord. During those days, if a boy was born to a family from the tribe of Levi, the Levite family hid their son for three months. When they could no longer hide him, by faith, they launched the child in a basket upon the waters expecting to see God's divine providence come forth.

Pharaoh's daughter found one of these baskets caught in the bulrushes and claimed the child she found there as her own son. It was she who named him Moses, meaning "drawn from the water." Moses' sister Miriam, who watched this entire scene unfold, offered their own mother's services as a nurse. The Bible says his mother nursed him until the time he was brought to the palace to be trained as the son of Pharaoh's daughter.

The plan of God was in motion. Moses was trained in the affairs of the Egyptians, learning their ways and their language. When he was grown, he observed the struggles of his brethren, the Israelites. He killed an Egyptian while defending one of them. When Pharaoh found out, he sought to slay Moses. Rather than face Pharaoh's wrath, Moses fled to Midian, came upon a well, and was content to stay. There he married one of the daughters of Jethro, the priest of Midian and tended his flock for 40 years.

As a shepherd, Moses had plenty of time to think. I believe Moses sensed the plan and purpose God had for his life and saw himself as a deliverer. He tried to carry out that plan in defending the Israelite that was being oppressed by the Egyptian. However, his perception was small compared to God's <u>large plan</u>. Moses was not ready at the palace because he was operating in his own strength. In his own strength what could he have done? For all his days in the desert, Moses likely questioned God and himself. Had he missed God's plan of deliverance for his people? Was he even a part of that plan? Many of us have been in this position, and thought we were in the plan of God but found ourselves in a spiritual wilderness. However, Moses' example shows that this experience is not for naught.

During Moses' stay in the desert, he was given the huge responsibility of caring for his father-in-law's flock. It was truly a time of preparation. A loving shepherd has a 24-hour a day job. He protects his sheep from predators, leads them to green pastures for nourishment and makes sure none wander off. The shepherd must also make sure the sheep don't get too comfortable, for when sheep lie down, gases build up in their stomach causing them to roll onto their back. Their legs go straight up in the air making it impossible for them to turn right side up again. This is called a *cast* sheep. If the shepherd doesn't come to the rescue, the sheep will die. Moses needed to learn how to care for GOD'S SHEEP. He needed to develop the heart of a shepherd before he could be the deliverer of God's people.

Chapter 2: In His Presence

As I meditated on Moses, I realized the word says Moses *led the flock to the backside of the desert and came to the mountain of God.* I think that was prophetic. In time he did that very thing with the people of God. When the Angel of the Lord appeared to him out of a flame of fire, Moses said "I must turn aside now and see this marvelous sight, why the bush is not burned up."

Moses stopped focusing on the sheep, the things that were around him on a daily basis, and he looked in a different direction. He looked toward God, not toward himself. Once He turned toward God, then the Lord called and said "Moses, Moses." All that Moses experienced up to this point was for the CALL of God. Moses might have missed his opportunity to know God and receive His instruction if he had not turned aside to see God.

If you look at all the heroes of faith, they all had one thing in common. They <u>**knew God.**</u> They had a face to face relationship with Him. In Psalm 103:7 it says, "He made known His ways unto Moses and His acts unto the children of Israel."

Our goal should be to know the ways of God the way that Moses came to know the ways of God. Exodus 33:11 tells us that "The Lord spoke to Moses face to face as a man speaks to a friend." In Exodus 33:14 God told Moses, "My presence (paniym) shall go with thee."

In Numbers 12 we read an account where Miriam and Aaron criticized Moses for marrying an Ethiopian woman. They said, "Is it true that God has only spoken to Moses? Hasn't He spoken with us too?" The Lord heard their conversation. In verse 3, it says "Now the man Moses was very meek above all the men who were upon the face of the earth." The word "meek" there isn't a shy, depressed personality; it is an attitude of the heart. One translation says "He preferred to suffer wrong rather than do wrong."

It's a character trait learned in the presence of God.

The Lord called Moses, Aaron and Miriam to meet with Him. He addressed Miriam and Aaron and said, "Listen to what I say: when there is a prophet among you, I, Adoni, make myself known to him in a vision, I speak to him in a dream. **But it isn't that way with my servant Moses.** He is the only one who is faithful in my entire household. With him I speak **face to face.**"

IN THAT WE FIND THE KEY - God is after your heart. All that matters to God is a CLEAN HEART in faithful submission to Him.

Jeremiah 9: 23-24 reveals God's desire:

"Thus sayeth the Lord, Let not the wise man glory in his wisdom neither let the mighty glory in his might, neither let the rich man glory in his riches, but let him that gloryeth, **glory in this**: that he understands and knows ME, that I am the Lord which exercises lovingkindness, judgment and righteousness in the earth."

David, like Moses, was another man after God's own heart. He began as a shepherd boy whose heart was fixed on the Lord. **David knew God.** There is a thread we see in all God's men and woman of faith. What they all have in common is that *they know God.*

Chapter 2: In His Presence

David defended his people against a giant with a sling shot and some stones. In the natural that looked pretty silly to the giant who was dressed in full battle array. David was confident, however, because he knew the Lord his God would deliver them. The enemy's challenge to us is the same today. He stands against us with all the accoutrements of warfare, the situations and circumstances of life. You can't use natural weapons in a spiritual battle. Our victory is through our faith in God to deliver on His Promises, not in our own abilities.

All God requires of us is to do justly, and to LOVE mercy and to walk humbly with thy God.

Chapters

Obedience, the Fruit of Faith

In His Presence

God's Secret Weapons

Identity Theft

Who Are We?

You Can't Kill a Dead Man

The Storehouse of Special Wealth

Chapter 3

God's Secret Weapons

The Lord told me a few years ago that He had secret (hidden) weapons. He reminded me of Elijah in the book of I Kings where He said, "I have 7,000 reserved for myself." Paul recounts this in Roman 11:4, "All the knees of which have not bowed unto Baal and every mouth which has not kissed him."

When you kiss someone, there are two things that happen. You are face to face in intimacy and reflecting that image. The word kiss means to fasten as with an attachment. What is it we attach? We attach our words and thoughts. When we mull over and think on what the enemy says, we enter intimacy with the enemy and conform to the enemy's thoughts and image.

We don't realize the importance of our words! The kind of person God is looking for is as Timothy put it, "blameless." This is not to say that we don't all miss it now and then, but the Lord is looking for a faithful heart that is fixed on Him, like the husband of one wife, or a "ONE woman man." It means having eyes only for one. It is a heart that doesn't wander.

That was the problem with Israel; they put their eyes on something other than the Word of God. I've heard it said our eyes are portals to the soul. I also believe your heart will follow that on which your eyes are fixed. Our focus must be on God alone so that our heart may be in covenant commitment with the Living God! We must not have a roving eye which begets a roving heart.

Paul exhorted Timothy concerning behavior in the house of God, which is the church, the pillar and ground of the truth. The CHURCH should be what upholds the TRUTH. In the garden, Adam had all the knowledge of what was good. It was when Eve attached her lips to what the enemy said and then acted on it that the knowledge of evil entered. It wasn't God's intention that we should know evil. But through grace God says, "I will put my laws into their hearts." The Lord has retained a remnant today, those that have the Laws of God in their hearts and His Word in their mouths. They are His secret weapons anointed by Him to fulfill the plan of God in this generation.

The anointing is the gift of the Holy Spirit given by God to equip men to accomplish His Will. The word Christ is not Jesus' last name. Christ means "anointing" which comes from another Greek word (Chrio) meaning to rub or smear with oil, also "to furnish," to consecrate, to furnish with the anointing. When a person accepts Jesus as Lord and the Holy Spirit comes into their life, He brings the anointing.

When we buy a house, most of the time it is empty and we have to furnish it. That's how we are when we are born again in Christ; we are clean but empty. The gifts and callings of God were declared before the foundations of the earth, but God furnishes us the same way we take great pains to decorate each room. The Father manifests the gifts and talents through a process of growth. It is Him working in you to do and to will His good pleasure. He has furnished us with the earnest down payment of the Holy Spirit, but it is up to us to yield to His will and do His pleasure. What is His pleasure? His pleasure is that we would comprehend who He has made us to be and use the gifts and talents He has given us to take dominion over the renegade spirits.

The anti-Christ is the spirit of lawlessness, a renegade and an enemy of the saints. "Anti" means against or opposing. It opposes the anointing of God. The enemy hates the anointing on a believer's life. He hates the person who is in covenant because when a person is united in one accord with God, ALL things are possible. The unity between two believers or between a believer and the Lord is All-powerful. That's why God had to divide the people with many languages at Babel. He said "in one accord they can accomplish anything." This one sentence is the key to success!

Lucifer had the anointing *once, before he fell from his position as an angel of God (cherub, guard of deity).* The anointing BELONGS TO GOD; it is part of Him. God assigns the anointing to positions and offices, not to individuals. When Lucifer lost the office, he lost the anointing. I think this is where people have gone astray in the church. Many people have been frustrated because they can't flow in certain gifts. They cannot flow in certain gifts because they are not appointed by God to do so. They have not been taught that the anointing is on the office, and if they are not assigned to that office, they will not be anointed to perform in that position. "Unless the Lord build a house, they labor in vain that built it." You can get it built, but the anointing won't be on it.

God's War Chest

Paul operated in his anointing to exhort Timothy in how to lead the church. He instructed Timothy not to give heed to myths, legends or genealogies which engender strife. He was instead to teach three things: to love out of a pure heart, to maintain a good conscience, and develop real, not nominal, faith. To have absolute, unfeigned faith equals total covenant with God. Are you in total covenant? Has your "yeah," been "yeah?" Have you given your word and kept it to your own hurt? (Ps 15:1-5) SELAH

Chapters

Obedience, the Fruit of Faith

In His Presence

God's Secret Weapons

Identity Theft

Who Are We?

You Can't Kill a Dead Man

The Storehouse of Special Wealth

Chapter 4

Identity Theft

In Genesis 1:14-16 God said, "let there be lights in the expanse of heavens to separate day from night and let them be signs for seasons, days and years."

THIS WAS GOD CREATING TIME: a segment in which we live. God doesn't start something and try to finish it. He finishes it and moves forward from there. Years ago we would say "everything starts in the spirit before it manifests in the flesh. We stopped short of realizing it **started and finished** <u>*before time existed*</u>. We just have to find out what God has done and exercise our faith to bring GOD'S will into this time frame.

Jesus said <u>before</u> He went to the cross, "Father, I've **finished** the work you sent me to do," *because in the eternal it was finished.*

IMAGINE ETERNITY, the expanse of never-ending. God just took a block, a segment of eternity to manifest His plan. A block or segment *we call* "TIME."

Eternity has no beginning and no end. The Word only gives us glimpses of before the creation of man, but we know GOD WAS and we know the enemy was here. I want you to stop here and really think about that.
See as God sees!

I want to take you back now to the beginning of "time." When we read the chronological Bible we see how the events happened in the order they occurred. Let's get a clearer picture of the facts.

In the beginning was the Word, and the Word was with God, and the Word was God. He was with God in the beginning (complete Jewish Bible). It tells us in Psalm 90, *"Before the mountains were brought forth, or ever thou had formed the earth and the world, even from everlasting to everlasting, Thou Art God."*

In Genesis 1:1-2 it reads, "In the beginning God created the heavens and the earth." Prior to this, everything was spiritual, because God is a spirit.

In Genesis 1: 11-12 God says "Let the earth bring forth grass the herb yielding seed, and the fruit tree yielding fruit after his kind whose seed is in itself, upon the earth: and it was so. And the earth brought forth grass and herb yielding seed after his kind and the tree yielding fruit whose seed was in itself after his kind: and God saw that it was good. And the evening and the morning were the THIRD day. Could this be when God planted the Tree of Life?

When we look at Ezekiel, we see that the enemy was already on the earth:

"You put the seal on perfection; you were full of wisdom and perfect in beauty, you were in Eden, the garden of God; covered with all kinds of precious stones. Carnelians, topaz, diamonds, beryl, onyx, jasper, sapphire, green feldspar, emeralds; your pendants and jewels were made of gold, prepared the day you were created. You were a **cherub** protecting a large region; I

Chapter 4 : Identity Theft

placed you on God's Holy Mountain. You walked back and forth among the stones of fire" (Ezekiel 28:12-13).

This is a description of Lucifer. He was in the garden, covered with precious stones. He wore a breastplate similar to the one God told Moses to make for Aaron the High priest to represent the 12 tribes of Israel, with one exception. Lucifer's breastplate had only 9 stones. Could they have represented the 9 orders of angels?

The meaning of the word cherub is, "winged celestial being" and are referred to in scripture as guarding God's presence. You find them above the ark covering the Mercy seat. In Genesis they are sent to guard the Tree of Life with flaming swords. **This order of angels, also known as cherubim, was used to guard deity.**

Lucifer, the word says, was set by God to protect a large region. Scripture says he was on God's mountain, in Eden and walked among the stones of fire. Prior to the rebellion in heaven Lucifer was the one in authority and God had set him there.
But **there was a war in heaven:** Michael and his angels fought against the dragon. The dragon and his angels fought Michael's angels, and prevailed not; neither was their place found any more in heaven. And the great dragon was cast out, that old serpent called the Devil, and Satan which deceiveth the whole world: he was cast out into the earth, and his angels were cast out with him.

The Word says, "You were perfect in the day you were created until **iniquity** was found in you." This word "iniquity" from the root means to distort, moral evil, unrighteous. "By the multitude of thy **merchandise** they filled you with violence and thou has sinned" (Revelation 12:7-9, 15-16). Interestingly enough the word "merchandise" means: to travel for trading as a peddler. Lucifer had peddled his distorted thinking to the angelic host and sin entered him and he would now be called the deceiver. Satan wanted to be God, and tried to be like God by using his Words.

Isaiah 14:12-14, (AMP) "How art thou fallen from heaven O Lucifer, son of the morning! How art thou cut down to the ground, you who weakened and laid low the nations? O blasphemous satanic king of Babylon, you *said in your heart,*
I will ascend to heaven
I will exalt my throne above the stars of God
I will sit upon the mount of assembly in the uttermost north
I will ascend above the heights of the clouds
I will make myself like the most high

Psalm 48:1-2 tells us that God sits high above the clouds. Satan's words demonstrate that his ultimate goal was to exalt his throne above the angels, Jesus, and God himself.

But Lucifer was <u>created</u> an anointed cherub. He was <u>not</u> created in God's image, only man was given that privilege. Man was given the ability to create. Lucifer was not. He was only able to form a hierarchy out of something already created, but God creates something out of nothing. His perfectness and position caused him to fall. He led a rebellion in heaven and was cast down to earth.

Chapter 4 : Identity Theft

"*The earth was unformed and void, darkness was on the face of the deep.*" Genesis 1:2

The word darkness here comes from the Hebrew root word, "choshek" which means to withhold light, also means misery, destruction and death. This is a picture of what Lucifer had become. In Ezekiel 28:16, God said to Lucifer "I will cast thee as profane out of the mountain of God." Therefore Lucifer who had been a cherub or *"guard of Deity"* fell from heaven and lost the ability to be over God's creation.

What was it that happened to God's Garden? Now if the earth had been God's garden before Lucifer fell, we can see his presence caused the GREAT darkness. Just imagine one who thought he was God and had the ability to be like God, couldn't reverse the darkness.

In Genesis it reads, "the Spirit of God moved upon the face of the waters" and God SAID, "Let there be light." God continued to create the place where God would put His man, one *who was like God* and had God's creative ability and authority. We see a place of provision and protection. Adam was given a position of authority to guard the garden, the place of God's Presence.

God was making a new creation, one who was like Himself. He placed Adam in the garden with the Tree of Life. The root word for life in Hebrew is "chay" and is the root of "chayah" which means TO REVIVE (Strong's 2416, 2421).Webster's definition of revive is "to return to life or consciousness, to return to health or vigor, to bring back into use."

God was restoring His garden. In Genesis 2:15, "the Lord God took man and put him into the Garden of Eden to <u>*dress*</u> it and to <u>*keep*</u> it."

Dress is the word "abad," meaning "to serve, to keep in bondage" (Strong's 5647). Man was to keep the earth in bondage, under the rule of God. Keep is the word "shamar" meaning "to hedge about, to protect, and to guard" (Strong's 8104).

God gave Adam and Eve COMPLETE AUTHORITY over the garden. God had also instructed them to guard and defend the garden. His use of the words "guard" and "defend" directly implies that there is an enemy in the earth, but man has authority over him.

This enemy hates man because man took his place. <u>*The authority and position of being the guard of deity was given to us.*</u> The Tree of Life was God's presence and Adam was given responsibility to guard and protect it. But there was another presence there that fit the description of a fallen angel. It was described as the Tree of the Knowledge of Good and Evil.

Ezekiel 28:12b "thus says the Lord God; thou sealest up the sum, full of wisdom and perfect in beauty.

The Word of God teaches us in pictures. Trees are used to represent man in the word. So, if the tree of Life was God's presence, who was described as being full of wisdom and knowledge? Lucifer. The tree of the knowledge of good and evil was a picture of Satan.

God gave man dominion over all the earth. They had God's presence with them, all their needs were supplied, and they were created in God's image. **They had authority and the ability to create with their words the same as God.** He gave them **one**

Chapter 4 : Identity Theft

charge, **one** command: not to eat of the Tree of Knowledge of Good and Evil. Of all the other trees they may freely eat.

Now the serpent was more subtle than any beast of the field which the LORD God had made. And he said unto the woman, Yea, hath God said, ye shall not eat of every tree of the garden?

And the woman said unto the serpent, we may eat of the fruit of the trees of the garden:

But of the fruit of the tree which is in the midst of the garden, God hath said, ye shall not eat of it, neither shall ye touch it, lest ye die.

And the serpent said unto the woman, ye shall not surely die:

For God doth know that in the day ye eat thereof, then your eyes shall be opened, and ye shall be as gods, knowing good and evil. And when the woman saw that the tree was good for food, (LUST OF THE FLESH) and that it was pleasant to the eyes, (LUST OF THE EYES) and a tree to be desired to make one wise, (PRIDE OF LIFE) she took of the fruit thereof, and did eat, and gave also unto her husband with her; and he did eat.

The Lord God said to the serpent, because you have done this thing you are cursed, I will put enmity between thee and the woman and between thy seed and hers.
(Genesis 3:14-15)

ENMITY translates WAR…God declared war!

At this point Adam and Eve surrendered their authority to Satan because of their disobedience to God. The devil has NO NEW TRICKS and while he may have won that battle, it is our responsibility to guard and defend our garden, our heart, mind, and body from Satan's whispers, hisses, and temptations. Interestingly enough, Satan had been looking for the promised man that would bruise his head since the garden. Now we read in Matthew Chapter 3 the appearance of John the Baptist and Jesus' baptism in the river Jordan. As Jesus came up out of the water the heavens were opened and John saw the Spirit of God descending like a dove, and alighting on Jesus, and a voice from heaven saying, *"this is my beloved Son in whom I am well pleased."*

This is just what Satan was looking for; finally he saw the promised seed, the one who will bruise his head. God had just spoken "THIS IS MY BELOVED SON." So what is the first thing the enemy does?

The enemy questioned Jesus' IDENTITY. In Luke 4, we see an almost identical attack by the devil for authority with the temptation of Jesus in the wilderness. Luke accounted for the temptation of Jesus in the three areas of life, lust of the flesh, eyes and pride of life. But the most deceptive maneuver was Satan's first word in his approach to Jesus, "IF thou be the son of God."

"If thou be the Son of God command these stones to be made bread." (Lust of the flesh)

Jesus replied, "IT IS WRITTEN, man does not live by bread alone, but by every word that proceeds out of the mouth of God." In a later conversation, Jesus told his disciples, "I have bread you know not of," speaking of His intimacy with the Father.

Chapter 4 : Identity Theft

Then the enemy offered him all the kingdoms of the world in a moment of time. Satan's offer was just for the kingdoms in this block of eternity called time. Jesus' Kingdom is forever!

He said, "All this power will I give thee and the glory of them, for it has been delivered to me and to whom I will give it, IF you will worship me, all shall be yours." (Lust of the eyes)

Jesus responded, "Get behind me Satan, for it is written, 'Thou shall worship the LORD thy God and him only shall thou serve."

The battle between God and Satan was for the rulership of worship. The word says, "To whom you yield your members to obey THAT'S whose servant you become." When you believe the enemy over God, you have given worship to the enemy.

"Then he brought him to Jerusalem and set him on a pinnacle of the temple, and said unto him, IF THOU BE THE SON OF GOD, cast thyself down. For it is written, He shall give His angels charge over thee, to keep thee and in their hands they shall bear thee up, lest thou dash thy foot against a stone. (Pride of life)

Jesus answered, "Thou shall not tempt the Lord thy God." *The Father had just said Jesus was HIS SON.* The enemy was tempting Jesus on whether he BELIEVED what God had said. He was questioning Jesus' **identity**, the same way he questions yours.

The most deceptive maneuver of the enemy is vying for your position just as he did with Jesus. He was questioning Jesus identity just like he questions yours! Satan's goal is still the same, he is still trying to exalt his word and will above God. He knows he already lost the battle with God and knows Jesus stripped him of all authority and power and given it to us! He knows dominion and authority was given to man. So to gain authority he NEEDS OUR WORDS.

> JESUS HAD A CHOICE, AND SO DO WE.
> WHOSE REPORT WILL YOU BELIEVE?

Chapters

Obedience, the Fruit of Faith

In His Presence

God's Secret Weapons

Identity Theft

Who Are We?

You Can't Kill a Dead Man

The Storehouse of Special Wealth

Chapter 5

Who Are We?

If we are going to talk about Identity Theft we have to ask ourselves, "Who are We?" To find that out we go to Genesis 1:1, "In the beginning GOD CREATED." In Hebrew, the phrase is, Elohiem Bara, meaning, "the Creator creating something out of something that doesn't exist!"

In Genesis 1, God **said**, "Let there be light; let there be firmament; let the earth bring forth grass, the herb yielding seed and the fruit tree yielding fruit," and it was so. The earth brought forth. Everything was created to produce after its own kind. In verse 26, God said "Let us make man in our image after our likeness." **God is a Prophetic speaker;** He created everything by His WORD.

Man, who is made of God's seed, **was created to be like God on the earth. We were created in His image and have God's Identity!** Since we are like God, we have the power to create with our words. The Word says, "God speaks those Things that be not as though they were." When we choose to accept the words of the enemy and act on them we give rulership to Satan in our lives.

Satan is after our position in Christ. He can't be God so he pursues your position of authority and identity. The way he does it is by deception. The enemy knows our confidence is in God's Word, so he has to undermine what God **has** said by introducing thoughts that are contrary to God's Word.

We have to always remember we were not purchased with silver and gold, but with the precious BLOOD of JESUS. The promises of God are YES AND AMEN to those that BELIEVE. There is one contingency; you must believe.

In the Merriam-Webster Dictionary, believe means "to accept the word or evidence as being true." You must accept God's Word regarding His character, integrity and faithfulness as a constant. He is not a man that He can lie or the son of man that He can repent, or change His mind about Who He is.

However, each of us has a soul that has a will and emotions. We are not constant in that realm. Our emotions fluctuate with circumstances. We have a good day and we feel great. God loves us and we're on good terms with the world. Situations arise and all of a sudden because of our emotions we feel depressed and forsaken by God.

God didn't change, in that moment; we did. The Word instructs us in Second Corinthians 10:3-5 to "cast down imaginations and to take every thought captive and bring it into obedience of Christ." This is why it is so important to learn to discern by the Word, what is good and evil. Only through the Word of God can we assimilate what ARE right thoughts and how to control our emotions.

Chapter 5: Who Are We?

Example:

- Your symptoms say you are sick.
- God's Word says we were healed by the stripes on Jesus back.
- Your situation says you have lack.
- God's Word says we are blessed and prosperous.
- You feel that circumstances control your life.
- God's Word says you reign in life.

The enemy is still trying to exalt his word above God's; however, the Promises of God are YES AND AMEN! The Word also says "He ALWAYS causes us to triumph in Christ." That's because the battle has already been won. It's now up to us to BELIEVE.

The church has done herself a disservice, by being moved by emotions, instead of what God **has already said.** If you look at all the great moves of God they came out of a man or woman who believed in what God had promised and acted upon it. Hearing what God has said or God is saying allows us to produce.

There are many in the body of Christ who are discouraged. To be "discouraged" is to have LOST COURAGE. But the Word says "Be of good courage and He will strengthen your heart, all ye that believe" (Psalm 31:24).

The word "believe" appears 143 times in the New Testament. We as the body of Christ <u>must</u> believe what God has said and act on it to manifest the desired results. God has given us the keys to the Kingdom and all authority in this world, but also the **responsibility** that goes with our rights and privileges.

When we are in right standing with God the Word says that He hears us when we pray and sends the answers while we YET SPEAK.

When you stand praying, FORGIVE. When you pray, BELIEVE you have RECEIVED.

This is the confidence we have, that He listens to us whenever we ask anything **in accordance with His Will**. If we know that He listens to whatever we ask, we know that we obtain the requests we have made to Him. (I John 5:14) His Will is SALVATION or in Greek it is SOZO, which means, total restoration of the triune man.

Know that "whatever you pray for and ask, believe you have got it and you shall have it" (Mark 11:24). When we don't see the answer to our prayer, sometimes we are moved by our natural thinking and emotions. We then think we have to twist the arm of God to do something, when He already has made the provision. We are inclined to believe how we feel over what God has said, thereby making our thoughts and emotions gods of our life. **Our bodies are not an indicator of truth.**

What is the reality and what is the truth?

The war over reality started for us in the garden. We all know we are at war; the Bible is clear about that. It says, "We wrestle not against flesh and blood" and "to put on the whole armor of God". We wouldn't need armor if we were in Paradise. I think for too long we have been as one that "beateth the air." We lost sight of what we were fighting for and who we were to fight with. We forget that "the devil is a liar and the father of lies"

Chapter 5: Who Are We?

(John 8:44). The sin nature that entered man in the garden darkened his perception of reality. Adam became a bond slave to Satan. The reality he once knew was becoming a faint memory. The Bible says that the whole earth was cursed because of Adam's fall.

We saw the enemy's mind set of the five "I WILLS." God's plan in the garden was a blessing, but Lucifer challenged the reality of God's Word. Not only did he question their identity, when he started with "Hath God said…" but he also questioned the reality of God's Word. We have been at war ever since.

Reality is made up of what we <u>know.</u> To an Eskimo, dog sleds, igloos, ice fishing are reality. To an NYC businessman, traveling on subways and walking crowded streets may be reality. Whatever we know and agree with is what reality is to us. So let's PREPARE for war, not only for the battles, but for the VICTORY.

This is why God wants us to KNOW HIM and agree with HIS WORD. In Genesis 11:6, God himself said, "Whatever mankind imagined it had the potential to accomplish."
THAT'S REALITY!!!

We should recognize that the Greeks when writing the New Testament had no word for "reality." To them truth and reality were of the same essence.

The weapon God has given us to combat the lies of the enemy is the Word of God. Jesus said His words are spirit and are life. In 1980, the Lord told me the only vehicle that connects this world with the spirit realm is words.

Jesus said that he would send us the comforter, the Spirit of truth. The world cannot receive Him, because it does not see or know Him, but you know Him, because He remains with you and will be in you. This point is essential; in our war over who controls man's world, the singular weapon God has given the church is HIS SPIRIT-EMPOWERED WORD. HIS WORDS ARE SPIRIT AND THEY ARE LIFE.

The Living word of the Spirit *is* the Truth. A high price was paid for you and me to walk in this position in Christ. It was the BLOOD OF JESUS. Even in the Old Testament the type of the blood was enough to protect and deliver the children of Israel.

In Exodus 12 we see the blood put over the doors and lentils of the children of Israel which saved them from the angel of death. We see the SCARLET CORD hanging out of Rahab's window spare her and her family from the attack on Jericho. Even a representation of the Blood was enough. So imagine the BLOOD OF CHRIST which is continually poured out for us being any less effective. The Blood has NEVER lost its power. The price was paid for sin, sickness and peace. The presence of His spirit was already made available to us again through HIS blood. So we must be attentive to the Word when it says, "Know ye not that to whom ye yield yourselves to obey, his servants ye are to whom ye obey, whether of sin unto death, or of obedience unto righteousness?" Of what tree **are** you eating?

WHOSE WORDS ARE YOU PARTAKING OF?

Chapters

Obedience, the Fruit of Faith

In His Presence

God's Secret Weapons

Identity Theft

Who Are We?

You Can't Kill a Dead Man

The Storehouse of Special Wealth

Chapter 6

You Can't Kill a Dead Man

Through disobedience, man was brought under a curse of death. But God counteracted the law of death with the impartation of His OWN Spirit in us to bring us to Life.

"Christ hath redeemed us from the curse of the law, being made a curse for us: for it is written, Cursed is every one that hangeth on a tree: That the blessing of Abraham might come on the Gentiles through Jesus Christ; that we might receive the promise of the Spirit through faith."
Galatians 3:13-14

"Know ye not, that so many of us as were baptized into Jesus Christ were baptized into his death? Therefore we are buried with him by baptism into death: that like as Christ was raised up from the dead by the glory of the Father, even so we also should walk in newness of life. For if we have been planted together in the likeness of his death, we shall be also in the likeness of his resurrection: Knowing this, that our old man is crucified with him, that the body of sin might be destroyed, that henceforth we should not serve sin. For he that is dead is freed from sin. Now if we be dead with Christ, we believe that we shall also live with him: Knowing that Christ being raised from the dead dieth no more; **death hath no more dominion over him."** Romans 6:3-9

Galatians 2:20 says "I was crucified with Christ, nevertheless I live, yet not I, but Christ liveth in me: and the life which I now live in the flesh, I live by faith of the Son of God, who loved me and gave himself for me."

It is no longer I that live, but Christ lives in me! It is no longer I that live; it is His image on the inside of me. The Word says, "God Always causes me to triumph in Christ Jesus." Why, *because, my life is hid in Christ.*

God created man out of the dust of the earth and gave him a flesh body. We read in Hebrews, "Wherefore when he cometh into the world he saith, sacrifice and offering thou wouldest not, but a body thou hast prepared for me" (Hebrews 10:5).

Charles Capps says, "Our bodies are nothing more than earth suits." When astronauts travel to the moon they need a space suit. **To live on this planet, you need a body (an earth suit).** Isaiah 59:16 speaks of Jesus, saying "and he saw there was no man and wondered there was no intercessor, therefore HIS arm brought salvation unto Him and His righteousness sustained Him." God didn't need any more sacrifices, a BODY was necessary to gain control again in the world.

John 10:1-3 says, "Verily, Verily I say unto you, he that enters not by the door into the sheepfold but climbs up some other way, the same is a thief and a robber. But He that enters in by the door is the shepherd of the sheep." Jesus came into this

Chapter 6: You Can't Kill a Dead Man

world with a flesh body. The door was opened by the Holy Ghost and the sheep hear His voice.

What Jesus is saying is the door to this world is a flesh body! SATAN NEEDS A BODY in order to operate in this realm. He gained access by Adam and he entered illegally. The enemy doesn't have a body, or a mouth to speak.

The only way he can bring to pass what he wants, is to <u>use your mouth</u>.

The Word says "I set before you life and death, blessing and cursing, therefore CHOOSE LIFE." Since the enemy has no authority to carry out his threat, he needs us to give him authority to do it. YOU HAVE CREATIVE ABILITY TO GIVE LIFE OR DEATH TO IMAGINATIONS.

II Corinthians 10:3-5 states, "For though we walk in the flesh we do not war after the flesh: For the weapons of our warfare are not carnal but mighty to the pulling down of strongholds casting down imaginations and every high thing that exalts itself above the Word of God, and bringing into captivity every thought to the obedience of Christ."

The Word says the power is in our tongue. If we as believers understand this, we will stop waging war on ourselves. The soul is made up of our mind, will and emotions that have to be submitted to the Word of God. **Jonah 2:8 reads, "They that observe lying vanities forsake their own mercy." When we start to listen to what the enemy has to say over what God's Word says, we forsake our own mercy.**

Luke 19:10 says that Jesus came to seek and to save THAT which was lost. Identity is the thing that was lost. Reality is that the enemy has nothing in his tool kit except deception, doubt and fear. To use these he MUST undermine your identity.

Look once more in Genesis 3 where the serpent asks Eve, "Yeah, hasn't God said you can eat of every tree in the garden?" She answered him with the exact words of God's command, and Satan responded, "Ye shall not die, for God knows the day you eat thereof your eyes will be open and ye shall be as gods knowing good and evil." What the enemy said to her was the truth. If they ate of the tree they would know good and evil. Otherwise, if it wasn't true, there would have been no temptation. Eve made a conscious decision to disobey God. But, the word "gods" in the text is the word, Elohiem the creator creating.

THEY ALREADY WERE LIKE *"THE"* GOD of the universe. Eve didn't know who she was; she didn't know her identity! Because of her lack of understanding, Eve and Adam forfeited their authority. The knowledge of evil caused them to lose sight of who they were.

The enemy's tactics never change. A verdict and sentence has already been decided. Jesus was convicted guilty in our place, and we can't be found guilty of the charge. We are the righteousness of God in Christ Jesus! Bought and paid for by His blood. We are more than conquerors through him that loved us. The word says "we have overcome by the blood of the Lamb and by the word of our testimony."

Each soul is made up of a mind, a will and emotions; all of these must submit to the Word of God. We know the Word is filled with types and shadows and is illustrated by pictures for us to understand. I always found it interesting that Golgotha is

Chapter 6: You Can't Kill a Dead Man

called the place of the skull and is the place where the final blow of death occurred. My thought has always been that this is a picture of what has to die in us. Our thoughts that are contrary to the Word of God must die. The price was paid for us on Golgotha to take back control of our souls. The acceptance of Jesus as savior is all that is needed to get to heaven. But the Word says we have to work out our own salvation with fear and trembling. This is not salvation of our spirits but our SOULS, our mind, will, and emotions brought under obedience to Christ.

Revelations 6:9: "And when he had opened the fifth seal, I saw UNDER THE ALTAR the SOULS of them that were slain for the Word of God and for the testimony which they held."
I believe this can be taken literally and spiritually. These are they that submitted their thoughts, will and emotions in this life to the Word of God and died the death of self.

Paul wrote to Timothy, his son in the faith, "Thou therefore endure hardness, as a good soldier of Jesus Christ. No man that warreth entangleth himself with the affairs of this life; that he may please him who hath chosen him to be a soldier" (I Timothy 2:3-4). When I read that I hear Paul saying this is an all-volunteer army and there is only one requirement to join: DEATH. This means death of self and becoming a bond slave to the Lord.

Natural soldiers submit their will to the commander. When young men and woman join the armed forces today, they fully understand that they have to submit their mind, will and emotions to their superiors. I believe Paul used the terms of the military to help us understand the death of self that is required to be part of God's army. It means death to what you think, feel and hear, and a submission ONLY to hear and see what the Father says to do.

WE ARE GOD"S LAW ENFORCEMENT OFFICERS ON THIS EARTH. WE ENFORCE THE LAW OF GOD ON OUR ENEMIES.

I want to share something the Lord showed me a few years ago. I had been in ministry when the enemy advanced an all-out assault on my life. I left the church and was away from ministry for 12 years. One day in prayer the Lord gave me a vision of myself lying in a hospital bed in a coma for 12 years. It was as if I was alive, but dead.

I saw myself wake up and the Lord said to me, "it's time to get dressed in your armor and stand shoulder to shoulder with the army of God." In my mind's eye I saw myself slipping into battle gear, one piece at a time. First the Helmet of salvation, then the breast plate of Righteousness. Then I wrapped my loins, my mind, will and emotions in the word.

In the physical, our loins are the pro-creative ability that produces life. It is the same in the spiritual. Paul is saying our loins are the thoughts we produce and give life to. The creative ability in the spirit needs to be girded with the Truth of God's Word.

In the dream, I then slipped on my sandals of peace, that's the heart attitude of John the Baptist crying "repent for the kingdom of God is come nigh," and grabbed my SWORD. It was bright and shiny and I was ready for war. But this time I would be more prepared. Just then the Lord brought to my mind a prophecy someone gave me just before that onslaught.

Chapter 6: You Can't Kill a Dead Man

She said, "In prayer the Lord showed me that Satan has desired to sift you as wheat, but Jesus said to tell you he has prayed and you will overcome." I heard the Lord say, "That is the closest to death you will ever come." You see, death is not the cessation of this earthly life.

Death is separation from the presence of God. Life and death are of the spirit. Death is caused by our cessation of partaking of HIM. Jesus paid the price for us to regain our identity and walk in the creative authority Adam lost in the garden. Jesus FINISHED the work for our complete victory.

I once saw a vision of myself in a coffin, lifeless. The Lord and I stood by it together as we looked at my body. The Lord said, you confess my word that says, "I was crucified with Christ, nevertheless I live, yet not I, but Christ lives in me: and the life I now live in the flesh I live by the faith of the Son of God who loved me and gave himself for me. So, I have a question: could cancer kill this body? Can this body fear? If I slapped that body in the face would it be offended?"

I said, "No, Lord". He said, "Why not?" I said, _"You can't kill a dead man"_
He responded, "That's right, you confess your life is hid in Me and you were crucified and died with me; how can any of these affect you?"

Death has no more dominion over you. Jesus speaking to John on the Isle of Patmos said, "fear not, I am the first and the last: I am he that liveth and was dead and behold I am alive evermore; Amen and have the keys of hell and of death." Jesus also said while alive in the flesh, that "no man takes my life; I lay it down and take it up again."

Paul understood this revelation when he said, "For me to live is Christ and to die is gain. If I am to go on living in this body, this will mean fruitful labor for me. *Yet what I shall choose?* I do not know! For I am torn between two, having a desire to depart and be with Christ which is far better; but it is more necessary for you that I remain in the body."

We are Dead to sin, Dead to sickness, and Dead to this life. You can walk in the newness of the life. You have been delivered from the power of darkness and God has translated us into the kingdom of his dear Son, in whom we have redemption through his blood and even the forgiveness of sins.

As ye have received Christ Jesus, so walk IN HIM. (Col 1:13-14, Col 2:6)

GLORY BE TO HIS HOLY NAME FOREVER!!!!!

Chapters

Obedience, the Fruit of Faith

In His Presence

God's Secret Weapons

Identity Theft

Who Are We?

You Can't Kill a Dead Man

The Storehouse of Special Wealth

Chapter 7

The Storehouse of Special Wealth

The Holy Ghost is the treasure.

We started out studying God's War Chest. We learned a war chest is where the natural world houses the finances or stockpiles the equipment necessary for the proposed goal. God had a plan, a place where He would put His treasure.

In Exodus 19:5 God tells Moses, "Now therefore if ye will obey my voice indeed and keep my covenant, then ye shall be a peculiar (special wealth) treasure (this word treasure means storehouse) unto me above all the people; for all the earth is mine and ye shall be a kingdom of priests and a Holy nation."

God has called us to be a STOREHOUSE of Special Wealth, a dwelling place for His HOLY SPIRIT.

"Now if the ministry that brought death, which was engraved in letters on stone, came with glory, so that the Israelites could not look steadily at the face of Moses because of the Glory, fading though it was, will not the ministry of the Spirit be even more glorious?

For we do not preach ourselves, but Jesus Christ as Lord, and ourselves as your servants for Jesus' sake. For God who said " Let light shine out of darkness, made His light shine in our

hearts to us *the light of the knowledge of the glory of God in the face of Christ.*"
II Corinthians 3:7 and 4: 5-8

We have this TREASURE in jars of clay to show that this all surpassing power is from God and not from us. We need to discover that treasure, the deposit of wealth that is in our earthen vessels. In Colossians 1:25-27, Paul is talking about God's presence. He says:

"I became a servant according to the stewardship of God which was given to me for you, to fulfill the word of God, the *mystery* which has been hidden from the ages and generations, but now made known to His saints to whom God would make known the wealth of the glory of this *mystery* which is CHRIST IN YOU THE HOPE OF GLORY." (Wuest translation)

The word says God kept it a *mystery* because if the princes of this world knew they would not have crucified the Lord of Glory. *Glory is something we give to God and it literally translates to honor, praise and worship.*

Jesus' obedient life brought Glory to God, making Him LORD of worship, praise and Honor unto God. Remember, this is the same position that Satan was after. Jesus became the LORD OF GLORY, the supreme authority and controller of God's worship and praise. He took Lucifer's place.

Ephesians 3:16 states, "That He would grant you according to His RICHES IN GLORY, to be strengthened with might by His spirit in the inner man."

I always wondered what was meant by, "HIS RICHES IN GLORY." The word "riches" translates in the Greek to mean,

Chapter 7: The Storehouse of Special Wealth

supply, accomplish, to furnish, wealth, possessions, or a **valuable endowment**. Christ in us is the hope of Glory. It is a valuable endowment of Jesus' worship, praise and honor unto God that He has bestowed IN us.

We have not understood the **treasure** we have in us by the gift of the Holy Ghost. Yes, He is our comforter, Yes, He leads us and guides, Yes, He shows us things to come. But have we understood the value of having the endowment of JESUS' HONOR, PRAISE and WORSHIP unto God working in us?

Jesus is the LORD OF GLORY and has brought HONOR to God by His Worship of obedience to the Father and has sent us the answer for our VICTORY. Now we can understand why Christ in us is the Hope of Glory. It's the **anointing in us for Worship and praise that brings victory.**

You have to recognize the enemy's attempt to gain your worship of his thoughts, words and circumstances. The issues of life come on all of us, none are excluded. We need to be aware of the enemy's devices. As Satan sees we are standing on God's promises, he will always come to steal the Word from our hearts. He will turn the furnace SEVEN TIMES hotter than it should be turned. Or, he will like pharaoh take away your straw and demand more bricks. THAT'S THE TIME TO REJOICE, because you know he is giving it his last ditch effort to overturn you. KEEP YOUR EYES ON THE PRIZE. The mystery of God's riches in Christ is the ability to **rejoice in the midst of the trial. Then, you are assured of VICTORY.**

In the book of Mark, Chapter 4, Jesus spoke about the *mystery* of the Kingdom of heaven and how it is compared to a mustard seed. When it is sown it is less than all seeds, but when it grows up becomes greater than all herbs and shoots out great branches, so that the fowls of the air may lodge under its shadow. Jesus is the seed that was sown and the great branches are us. He is talking about the Church! Genesis revealed that every seed produces after its own kind. Jesus was revealing the *mystery*. Paul's letter to the Ephesians is so full of the revelation of this *mystery*.

"Blessed be God the Father of our Lord Jesus Christ who HATH blessed us with all spiritual blessings and hath chosen us in Him before the foundation of the world that we should be accepted in the beloved, in whom we have redemption in His BLOOD, hath abounded toward us in all wisdom and made known to us the *mystery* of His will purposed in Christ." Paul speaks of the mystery of Christ hidden for all ages past in God and NOW made known by revelation through the Spirit. The mystery is to bring all things in heaven and on earth together under one head, even Christ, who wants to bring us all under His anointing.

There are other mysteries in the Word. One is the mystery of iniquity, the hidden principle of rebellion against authority. Another is the mystery of Godliness: greater is He that is in you, than he that is in the world. Jesus said He had to leave, but would send the Comforter, The Holy Spirit to be our guide. The church needs to understand both, to be effective in this warfare. Religion has taught us that it's all about going to heaven to be with Jesus. When in reality it's all about His Spirit coming here and living in you. We were told we should live for Him. Does that mean we should be good little girls and boys and just make it into heaven? That's what the enemy would have you believe, but I DON'T THINK SO!

I John 4:2 reveals the truth:

"Hereby know ye the Spirit of God: every spirit that confesses that Jesus Christ is come in the flesh is of God."

That doesn't mean they confess a belief that He came in the flesh two thousand years ago, BUT that He is ALIVE in the flesh today "in us." The Hope we have isn't only that Christ will come someday, but that He is in us PRESENTLY to assure our victory. So many times I've heard Christians say, "Why are we here, to struggle through life and receive a heavenly reward?" NO! We are here for two reasons:

1. To reveal God the Father and His Son to a lost and dying world in our generation.

"Ye have not chosen me, but I have chosen you and ordained you, that ye should go and bring forth fruit and that your fruit should remain, that WHATSOEVER YE SHALL ASK the Father in my name he may give it you." (John 15:16)

2. We are here to enforce the law of God upon the enemy of our faith.

We have been given the same charge as Adam, to replenish the earth and subdue it. We are to reproduce spiritual children as well as natural. The word SUBDUE in Hebrew means to bring to bondage and conquer.

When the giant Goliath challenged all the mighty men of Israel, it took a shepherd boy with confidence to say, "God gave me the lion and the bear and this UNCIRCUMCISED Philistine will be as one of them, seeing he has defied the armies of the living God. The Lord that delivered me out of the paw of the lion and paw of the bear will deliver me out of the hand of this Philistine."

David declared the covenant, when he spoke to Goliath and said, "You come to me with sword, spear and shield; but I come to you in the name of the Lord of Hosts, the God of the armies of Israel whom you have defied."

"THIS DAY, WILL THE LORD DELIVER YOU INTO MY HANDS, so that all the earth may know that there is a GOD in ISRAEL." (I Samuel 17:46)

This was David's purpose, not to be famous, not to obtain the ransom, even though Saul offered him gifts, but to reveal God in the earth! This is why we declare, "I was crucified with Christ nevertheless I live, But the life I now live, I live by the faith of the Son of God who loved me and gave himself for me." (Galatians 2:20)

We were crucified with Him, suffered with Him, died with Him, buried with Him, justified with Him, made alive with Him, Conquered the enemy with Him, and RAISED to sit together with Him. The resurrection of Jesus is proof of our victory over the adversary.

"For the law of the Spirit of LIFE in Christ Jesus set me free from the Law of sin and death. Therefore death has no dominion over us."(Romans 8:2)

"All power has been given unto me in heaven and earth therefore you go in my name." (Matthew 28:18)

That's the concept Jesus was trying to convey to his disciples. "As He IS, so are we in this world." Jesus is VICTORIOUS. Thanks be unto God who *Always* causes me to

Chapter 7: The Storehouse of Special Wealth

triumph in Christ and makes manifest the savior of his knowledge by us, in every place.

Our sufficiency is of God who has made us able ministers of the New Testament, NOT of the letter, but of the Spirit, for the letter kills, but the Spirit gives Life. Now where the Spirit of the Lord is there is Liberty.

The same spirit that raised Christ from the dead dwells in us, and He translated us out of darkness into His marvelous light. Jesus is victorious so we are also victorious. The Old Testament tells us we will build Israel again. The word ISRAEL literally means "Soldier of God." The Old Testament charge is not to build a physical country, but a spiritual people!

The treasure of Israel that once made Himself real to His people in an Ark is now manifested in us.

The Ark of God was housed in the Holy of Holies and is also known as the Ark of the Covenant. It was God's actual presence in the wilderness that protected and made provision for them with a pillar of fire by night and a cloud by day. Designed by God to be carried by poles on the shoulders of men, this ark represented the way we carry His presence today. The Ark signified God's provision and protection and they were tangible manifestations of HIS PRESENCE.

We are the vessels that hold HIS TREASURE
WE ARE GOD'S WAR CHEST TODAY!

"Lord thou hast been our dwelling place in all generations. Before the mountains were brought forth, or ever thou hast formed the earth and the world, even from everlasting to everlasting, THOU ART GOD." (Psalm 90: 1-2)
Amen

"He made my mouth like a sharpened sword....He made me into a polished arrow." Isaiah 49:2

Notes

QUICK ORDER FORM

Name: _____
Address: _____
_____
City: _____ State: _____
Zip: _____
Telephone: _____
Email Address: _____

THERE ARE THREE WAYS TO ORDER PRODUCTS FROM Paula Vignali:
1 CALL toll free at <u>800-460-3037</u>and place your order over the phone.
2 FAX this order form to <u>800-460-3037</u> toll free phone / fax (Credit Card only).
3 MAIL this order form with a check/money order to: Paula Vignali
PO Box 106
Pluckemin, NJ 07978

Credit Card Info: (please circle the appropriate one)
Card Type: Visa   Master Card   Discover   Amex
Credit Card #: _____
Expiration Date: ____ / ____
3 and/or 4 Digit Code _____
Signature _____

Sales tax: I understand that 7% sales tax will be added to my order.
Shipping by air
U.S.: $4.00 for first book and $2.00 for each additional book.
International: $9.00 for first book; $5.00 for each additional book (estimate)
Please send more FREE information on: Yes / No (please circle the appropriate one)
   Other Books   Speaking/Seminars   Mailing Lists   Consulting

BLUEMAGICPUBLISHING.COM

QUICK ORDER FORM

Name: _____
Address: _____
_____
City: _____ State: _____
Zip: _____
Telephone: _____
Email Address: _____

THERE ARE THREE WAYS TO ORDER PRODUCTS FROM Paula Vignali:
1 CALL toll free at 800-460-3037 and place your order over the phone.
2 FAX this order form to 800-460-3037 toll free phone / fax (Credit Card only).
3 MAIL this order form with a check/money order to: Paula Vignali
PO Box 106
Pluckemin, NJ 07978

Credit Card Info: (please circle the appropriate one)
Card Type: Visa   Master Card   Discover   Amex
Credit Card #: _____
Expiration Date: ____ / ____
3 and/or 4 Digit Code _____
Signature _____

Sales tax: I understand that 7% sales tax will be added to my order.
Shipping by air
U.S.: $4.00 for first book and $2.00 for each additional book.
International: $9.00 for first book; $5.00 for each additional book (estimate)
Please send more FREE information on: Yes / No (please circle the appropriate one)
   Other Books   Speaking/Seminars   Mailing Lists   Consulting